W0010286

The Sagittarius
Woman

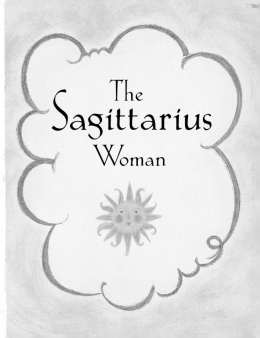

The Sag

Ariel Books

**Andrews McMeel
Publishing**

Kansas City

ittarius

Woman

November 23–December 21

Julie Mars

Illustrated by Sarah Hollander

ISBN: 0-7407-1439-2
Library of Congress Catalog Card Number: 00-106909

designed by Junie Lee
typeset by Ellen M. Carnahan

Contents

Introduction

Did you ever wish upon a star? Have you ever studied the night sky, transfixed by its vast beauty and magnificent mystery?

Astrologers believe that the celestial bodies overhead correspond in some significant way with our own bodies (and personalities) here on Earth.

For more than five thousand years, women have gazed heavenward, searching for connections between the cosmos and their own human minds and spirits. Looking to the planets and stars for guid-

ance in the areas of romance and friendship gives all women a powerful way to
understand and better direct their own
lives and personal destinies.

PLANETARY RULERS

Astrology is the product of centuries of
precise observation of both the planets
and human nature, yet it also incorpo-
rates a degree of intuition. So when an
astrologer identifies a sun sign, it is much
more than a convenient label. It is a
strong indicator of the particular cosmic

energy that helps shape each woman's personality. There even tends to be a natural affinity between two people born under the same planetary ruler.

Aries (March 21–April 20) is ruled by Mars, the planet of forcefulness, physical energy, and sex drive.

Taurus (April 21–May 21), like Libra, is ruled by Venus, the planet of love, affection, and pleasure.

Gemini (May 22–June 21), like Virgo, is ruled by Mercury, the planet of communication and travel.

Cancer (June 22–July 23) is ruled by the Moon, the planet of reflection, cyclical change, and receptivity.

Leo (July 24–August 23) is ruled by the Sun, the planet of self-centeredness, brilliance, and warmth.

Virgo (August 24–September 23), like Gemini, is ruled by Mercury, the planet of communication and travel.

Libra (September 24–October 23), like Taurus, is ruled by Venus, the planet of love, affection, and pleasure.

Scorpio (October 24–November 22) is ruled by Pluto, the planet of transfor-

mation through the powers of both creativity and destruction.

Sagittarius (November 23–December 21)
is ruled by Jupiter, the planet of good
luck, generosity, and success.

Capricorn (December 22–January 20) is
ruled by Saturn, the planet of hard
work, responsibility, and endurance.

Aquarius (January 21–February 19) is
ruled by Uranus, the planet of original-
ity, change, and sudden inspiration.

Pisces (February 20–March 20) is ruled
by Neptune, the planet of illusion, mystery, and the force of imagination.

ELEMENTS AND QUALITIES

Two other basic concepts are essential to astrological interpretation. The first is called the *element*, of which there are four: *earth, air, fire,* and *water.* Each element carries with it a vast body of associations that help you to understand how your sign interacts with other signs.

Earth. This element is often connected with such traits as steadiness, practicality, and predictability. "Earthy" women tend to be firmly rooted and notoriously stable. The three earth signs are Taurus, Virgo, and Capricorn.

Air. The signs associated with this element are more likely to be intellectual and analytical. "Airy" women tend to display great emotional detachment and are often described as elusive or unavailable. Gemini, Libra, and Aquarius are the three air signs.

Fire. This element is associated with activity, energy, and impulsiveness. "Fiery" women tend to be vivacious, dynamic, optimistic, and domineering. Aries, Leo, and Sagittarius comprise the three fire signs.

Water. This element is often associated with emotion and intuition. The water signs are Cancer, Scorpio, and Pisces. "Watery" women tend to be moody, sensitive, creative, and deep.

The final astrological variable is the *quality* of a particular sign. The quality reflects a sun sign's relationship to the rest of the world. There are three qualities: *cardinal,* which initiates change; *mutable,* which adapts to circumstances; and *fixed,* which maintains the status quo. Aries, Cancer, Libra, and Capricorn are outgoing, energetic cardinal signs. Taurus, Leo, Scorpio, and Aquarius are fixed, or resistant. Gemini, Virgo, Sagittarius, and Pisces are flexible, or mutable.

Each sign is a unique combination of quality and element. Because of this specificity, women can glean much personal information from even a minor astrological analysis. The complex art of astrology, with its mix of science and subjectivity, offers all women insight into the present ... and a hint or two about the future!

Just the Facts on Sagittarius

Motto: "I see"
Element: Fire
Quality: Mutable
Opposite Sign: Gemini
Ruling Planet: Jupiter
Animal: Horse
Jewel: Turquoise
Numbers: Five and seven

Your Sun Sign Profile

SAGITTARIUS

Imaginative, freedom-loving, and adventurous, the Sagittarius woman is likely to find herself on everyone's top ten list of best friends. Known for high spirits, gift of gab, and openheartedness, her charisma and confidence keep others coming back for more ... and more.

Astrologers often credit the female Water Bearer's oversupply of charm to her ruling planet, Jupiter. Sometimes called the Great Beneficent, Jupiter is most often linked with such superpositive attributes as optimism, abundance, expansiveness, and good luck. In ancient Roman mythology, Jupiter was the most powerful of the gods. His realm was the sky—and for today's Sagittarius woman, the sky is still the limit!

It's not unusual for the Sagittarius woman to travel light. Thoroughly committed to adventure and exploration (either mental or physical), she doesn't cling to material objects—or troublesome emotions, grudges, or disappointments.

She thrives when she feels completely free, and independence is her most cherished trait. And because she so values her own sense of freedom, she is not likely to inhibit others. She tends to stay out of other people's business, rarely (if ever) tries to control anyone else, and absolutely refuses to be manipulated.

Most Archer-women are philosophically inclined and determined to explore and broaden their horizons—over and over again. Each experience builds confidence and encourages her to face the next challenge, no matter how daunting it may appear to others.

And, of course, luck plays an important role in the drama of the typical Sagittarius woman. In fact, Sagittarians are often on intimate terms with the elusive Lady Luck. The female Archer takes risks, but she usually lands on her feet.

Kind, curious, and congenial, the Sagittarius woman enjoys her life and everyone in it, and the feeling is mutual!

Sagittarius and Friends

Sagittarius Woman/Aries Friends

Fire signs like to burn together—and the Archer and her Ram pals share many intellectual interests—and outdoor sports too! Plenty of fun is in store for these friends.

Sagittarius Woman/Taurus Friends

This friendship can lift off—if one rule is understood: There is no boss. Once Sagittarius and Taurus agree, the air is clear!

Sagittarius Woman/Gemini Friends

With Sagittarius's fire and Gemini's air, this friendship is like a furnace. It can heat up to a comfortable temperature—or blow up if it's out of balance!

Sagittarius Woman/Cancer Friends

Cancerians must be careful not to drown the Archer's fire. The Archer must not heat Cancerian water to a boiling point. Moderation is the key for lasting friendship.

Sagittarius Woman/Leo Friends

Extroverted, social, and fun-loving, the Archer is perfectly at home among the Lions. There's no size or scope limit to adventure for these mutually appreciative fiery friends.

Sagittarius Woman/Virgo Friends

No one will ever win the great order versus spontaneity debate. But the Archer and her Virgin pals should have a great time trying!

Sagittarius Woman/Libra Friends

Sagittarius is often called the best friend in the zodiac. And no friendship is more action packed and full of fun than the Sagittarius/Libra combination. Enjoy it!

Sagittarius Woman/Scorpio Friends

Sagittarius's irresponsibility and Scorpio's intense loyalty demands in friendship can result in a bumpy road. Both should exercise caution—or this fire/water combo could reach a permanent boil.

Sagittarius Woman Sagittarius Friends

Nothing can stand in the way of Sagittarians out for adventure. And there are no better partners for fun than each other. Full speed ahead!

Sagittarius Woman Capricorn Friends

Capricorn adores limits, Sagittarius has no consciousness of them. This leads to frustrations if the friendship is deep. So keep it superficial! Have some light-hearted fun!

Sagittarius Woman/Aquarius Friends

With their take-no-prisoners attitude toward fun, these two are perfectly paired for maximum excitement. And they can philosophize about it afterward too. A great friendship!

Sagittarius Woman/Pisces Friends

Put two mutable signs together—and both will desire a little stability. This friendship will have deep and satisfying moments, but it may not survive the long haul.

The Sagittarius Woman in Love

Adventure is her middle name . . . and, ultimately, what greater adventure can there be in life than a passionate romance? When she's plugged in to love, the Sagittarius woman positively crackles with fiery electricity. And she thoroughly warms those around her with her cheer, energy, and optimism.

But there's one small catch. The female Archer is more prone to fall in love than to stay in love. Her restless nature, her distaste for the inevitable emotional roller coaster of romance, and her essentially free spirit prevent her from burning with passion for too long . . . in one place.

The good news: She typically grows out of her romantic wanderlust. When the time is right, she throws herself into long-term love with a gusto unique to the great spirit of the Sagittarius woman.

Sagittarius Woman/
Aries Man

Put two human firecrackers together . . .
then stand back and watch the inevitable
pyrotechnics. If the couple happens to
consist of a Sagittarius woman and an
Aries man, the display tends to be quite
glorious and thrilling.

This is a pair in which each truly mir-
rors the other. They share the automatic
comfort of two similar personalities and
the challenge of a romantic partnership

in which action, adventure, and excitement are the most basic requirements.

Both the Archer-woman and the Ram tend to thrive in a social whirl. Boredom is their sworn enemy, and both are likely to run away from routine. Consequently, their romance will probably have many unexpected twists and turns—but each new wrinkle will likely only exhilarate them and bring them closer together.

With all their fire, passion will be no problem. The Sagittarius woman and the Aries man are well matched when it comes to love. Their red-hot romance may be momentarily cooled by the occasional temper tantrum, but these tend to blow over quickly—due, in part, to the Archer's eternal good cheer.

Other signs might have a problem with the Aries man's inclination to be self-centered and bossy. The Archer-woman typically thinks the Ram's little displays of egotism are adorable. Her sense of humor—and her high spirits—allow her to sail through these minor squalls.

Besides, these two never run out of things to talk about, and the more she talks, the more her Aries mate respects her. He sees the philosopher in her and likes it. He tends not to muse about life's meaning, and therefore he stands to learn a great deal.

With passion to burn and energy to spare, the Sagittarius/Aries match is made in the stars—and is destined to shine for a long, long time.

Sagittarius Woman/
Taurus Man

Taurus the Bull tends to be a creature of habit. Through hard work and determination, he builds his personal empire, and he enjoys adding to it day by day, bit by bit. Predictability and practicality are typically his favorite concepts, and accumulation is his ultimate goal.

Enter the footloose and fancy-free Sagittarius woman. She tends to dread routine in the exact proportion that the

Bull worships it. The female Archer is happiest when she's off on a madcap adventure or a quest for wisdom, and she tends to view experience as both the ends and the means to happiness. The Bull, on the other hand, measures progress by dollars in the bank or an increase in his general comfort—two things that rarely hit the Sagittarian's priority list.

The chance of a romantic meeting of the minds (or anything else) doesn't seem too promising. The Archer and the Bull are simply cut from different zodiacal cloth, and their differences are not superficial but deep. Should a Sagittarius woman fall for a Taurus man, she should expect moment-to-moment challenges and cherish the periods of harmony (or rest!) when they come.

One problem area is control. The Bull is a take-charge kind of guy. He can't help it. But the Sagittarius woman resents any tie that binds or even hinders her cherished freedom. If the Bull should stomp his feet or unleash his temper, the Archer will inevitably send a few verbal arrows zinging in his direction. They'll hurt, and the Taurus man won't recover quickly.

But the Sagittarius woman typically does not back off.

But there are always exceptions to romantic rules, and with major compromises on both sides, the female Archer and the Bull might make a go of it. Stranger things have happened in the realm of romance.

Sagittarius Woman/ Gemini Man

The typical Sagittarius woman is a born adventurer. Ruled by Jupiter, the planet of expansion, she is usually interested in broadening her horizons in every possible manner—and then philosophizing about it at length.

The ever-changeable Gemini man more than meets the Sagittarius woman's criteria for excitement, although hers is often a quest for understanding, while his might be centered on fun and games. Both the Archer and the Twins are restless by nature, and both love to talk: It's very likely that this fiery female and this airy male will ignite more than a spark of interest in each other.

Since both tend to be footloose by nature, neither is prone to pressure the other to settle down. And the Twins' dual nature keeps the Archer-woman guessing—which is exactly the kind of romantic stimulation she craves. But should she try to take control (and she probably will), the Twins may head for cover or perform their infamous disappearing act. When the Sagittarius woman acts like the boss, Gemini may give notice—effective immediately.

The Sagittarius woman typically desires deep meaning, and the Twins are known for skimming life's surface. This can cause clashes, and these clashes can escalate into all-out personal attacks. To avoid fireworks, both the Archer and the Twins are advised to focus on the fun and the freedom the other offers, and to learn to tolerate the differences that are really nothing more than minor romantic flak.

Opportunities for adventure with no strings attached are plentiful in this Sagittarius/Gemini pairing—and if one or the other should grow to desire a tie that binds, all it takes to make it happen is a bit of honest work. Not a bad romantic bargain by anyone's standards!

Sagittarius Woman/ Cancer Man

In stereotypical romantic role playing, the woman is the homemaker while the man strides confidently out to conquer the world. But this is one stereotype from yesteryear that needs to be thrown out— fast—if a Sagittarius woman and a Cancerian man should fall in love.

First of all, it's likely to be the Crab who craves security and stability. (Remember, his tough shell conceals a vulnerable interior.) For the typical Cancerian man, a sturdy, dependable home life is the foundation of happiness. He tends to be possessive and jealous, and he's not above criticizing (and even nagging) if he feels his all-important comfort is threatened.

With her deep love of independence, the Sagittarius woman is likely to resent his excessive demands for coziness. She thrives on journeys (mental or physical) and exploration, and sometimes even enjoys an extended period of recklessness. Cancer's caution may get on her nerves— but if she loads a verbal arrow into her bow and sets it flying in his direction, watch out! Her Crab will probably pout for weeks.

Optimism is a delightful trait of the Sagittarius woman, but not for the moody Cancerian man. He may feel temporarily scorched by her eternally sunny disposition. After all, he is a water sign and needs to go with the flow of his emotions. And she tends to be direct, while he, with Crab-like imprecision, rarely approaches any issue head-on. Both may grow frustrated.

But the news is not all bad! When it comes to romance, the Cancerian man can supply it with great creativity and sensuality; the Sagittarius woman, always on a quest for romantic perfection, knows a great thing when she sees it. She may very well compromise accordingly and reap the long-term benefits!

Sagittarius Woman/ Leo Man

Everyone is familiar with the wisdom of fighting fire with fire. But what about love and harmony? Is there any alchemy when it's passion, not combat, that is under discussion?

It's a well-kept secret that a fire/fire mating, as in the case of the Sagittarius woman and the Leo man, tends to be a natural romantic progression from warm to sizzling to white-hot. The Leo Sun, beaming good cheer and exuberance, and the Sagittarian Jupiter, expanding the general optimism, make a nearly unbeatable love combination.

Think about it: Who is best equipped to meet and satisfy the female Archer's passion for excitement? Who has enough self-confidence to applaud her love of freedom and release her from the grip of possessiveness or jealousy? Who has the fiery energy to accompany (or even lead) the Sagittarian woman on her quest for wisdom, understanding, and meaning?

Leo the Lion, of course. And in the

female Archer, the Lion finds a mate who can appreciate his need to be center stage, but is also ready to sidestep it as necessary, with grace and ease. Both are willing to take a risk—and both are typically graced by good luck, so neither will feel inhibited or restrained. In fact, neither is likely to cramp the other's style in any way at all.

This is delicious for the Sagittarius woman and the Leo man. The lack of emotional or psychological limits spills over into each aspect of their life together, and soon the Archer finds herself happily crossing into a whole new solar system of intimacy—with her Leo man at the center, just where he belongs and where he's happiest!

Some love matches are smooth; others are cosmic. The Archer/Lion combination has the potential to add new levels of meaning to the word *love*, while remaining free and easy too!

Sagittarius Woman/
Virgo Man

It's time for some astrological honesty. There are certain seemingly unavoidable problems between fire and earth signs. Blame it on the stars, but the impulsive energy that animates the fiery ones of the zodiac tends to terrify the practical, meticulous earth signs.

So it's no surprise that the fiery Sagittarius woman and the earthbound Virgo man may face a few romantic challenges.

To begin with, the Virgin tends to demand a sense of order in daily routine and in his emotional life too. He creates a place for everything (including passion), and he's content to see everything in its place—permanently.

This is very restricting for the Sagittarius woman. She tends to blaze a trail of glory across the hills and valleys of romance—and she neither looks back nor pays much attention to the warnings posted along the side of the road. This freestyle approach confuses the Virgin. He may shake his head, and if the Archer feels she's being judged—particularly by a man who exhibits signs of fear—she may let her arrows fly in his direction.

Of course, the Virgin is not actually afraid. He's just sensible and careful. But the Archer misses the point of such things. She flies by the seat of her pants, and the faster, the better. And she's more likely to leave a seemingly restrictive relationship than to enter one. This does not please the Virgin, who expects commitment once he surrenders to love.

But there is one area shining on their romantic horizon: the realm of the intellect. The Virgin analyzes, and the Archer philosophizes. A Sagittarius/Virgo pairing can be a great opportunity for a meeting of the minds—and if that's stimulating enough, they may put the fire/earth challenges on the back burner while true love blazes at the front of their hearts.

Sagittarius Woman/ Libra Man

Impetuous and often extravagant, the Sagittarius woman is typically a magnet for the attentions of the Libra man. She doesn't have to turn on the charm; it's just there—and he is sure to notice. For one thing, the Libra man, with his lusty curiosity, typically considers the female Archer fascinating. Her independent, restless ways and her passion for life's biggest gambles appeal to the part of him that's prone simply to stand back and observe a thing of extreme beauty.

While the Sagittarius woman can be a bit bossy, both she and the Libra man are ultimately followers of the live-and-let-live school. They typically feel a freedom together that suits them both. And given their tendencies toward the cerebral, the mind-to-mind talks can be thrilling, although the heart-to-hearts are often a bit more problematic. For the female Archer and the Scales, deep emotional drama is not particularly appealing.

With her great love of the outdoors,

animals, and the wilderness, the typical Sagittarius woman might wish for the same in a potential mate. The Libra man tends to avoid roughing it. He's typically more interested in a four-star hotel than a tent and a backpack. But he is as vivacious and expansive as she is, and with all that optimism to lean on, minor lifestyle problems can be worked out with no hard feelings.

But tread carefully in the realm of words! Libra is sometimes tactless, and Sagittarius can be painfully blunt. Both can dish it out, but neither can take it particularly well. It's best either to sidestep thorny issues or to develop the habit of apologizing (and forgiving) quickly.

Harmony is definitely in the air (and in the flames of passion) for this very promising fire/air romantic combination.

Sagittarius Woman/
Scorpio Man

A match between a typical Sagittarius woman and a typical Scorpio man is often accompanied by claps of thunder, flashes of lightning, and a downpour. It may be exciting once in a while, but when the weather stays the same for days, it can become exhausting—or even worse, boring.

Although the Sagittarius woman typically enjoys thrills and adventures, extended periods of high drama are rarely her emotional climate of choice. Consequently, the long-range outlook for this tempestuous duo is not among the most promising.

But what brings about the fire- and waterworks in the first place? Many things. For example, the Scorpio man is typically jealous and domineering. With his natural intensity, he thinks his demands are merely a demonstration of affection.

The Sagittarius woman is bound to bristle when she feels her precious freedom might be at stake. A large part of her Jupiterian joy comes from being expansive and open to all, which may not be possible if she finds herself hooked up with a Scorpio man. The Scorpion may insist that she close herself off to others and focus on him exclusively. To put it with Sagittarian bluntness, that's not likely to happen.

But if the Scorpion should sting, or if he retreats into a moody, watery isolation, the Archer will typically retaliate (remember, she has many arrows and the zodiac's strongest bow) or blaze off. She's rarely one to make the best of what she considers a bad bargain. Once she's safely at a distance, however, she'll probably make a few friendly moves in his direction. Meanwhile, the Scorpion, who doesn't forgive and forget, may occupy himself with plans for romantic revenge.

Passion for the short term or major personal adjustments (and frequent frustration) over time—these are the options for the Sagittarius woman and Scorpio man who chance to fall in love.

Sagittarius Woman/ Sagittarius Man

Take the best traits of the Sagittarius woman: generosity, cheerfulness, ambition, and optimism. Add in a Sagittarius man and the traits are multiplied by two. The result is a romantic match that has enough optimism and energy to burst the seams of love.

Now consider the wilder, less manageable side of the Sagittarian nature. It tends to lack staying power; it's excessively blunt (and simultaneously thin-skinned); it's outspoken and even bossy at times. What happens if those traits are doubled as well? Will the relationship roof blow off, or can romance burn on between these two fiery Archers?

There's a fine chance for long-term, mutual admiration here, partly because these two are so much alike. Both are independent and fun-loving, freedom minded and kind. Each understands the other's need to search for truth and wisdom, and each accepts the other's need to gamble—even with the relationship—

from time to time. And since "no strings attached" is the philosophy of choice, there are rarely fits of jealousy or possessiveness.

On the other romantic hand, one Sagittarius is often enough for any twosome. When the Sagittarian unpredictability, restlessness, and extravagance are doubled, the foundation of love can feel very weak, indeed. They may not admit it, but Sagittarians often need a bit of grounding in order to thrive in love. They search for it in a partner.

They probably won't find it together. But with all the encouragement and

optism of two Archers, they can probably create a substitute for security—one
that works for them in a unique but powerful way. Love is resourceful. The impetuous Archers may be able to build a
bond that ties them together, loosely but
permanently.

Sagittarius Woman/
Capricorn Man

Before we discuss the romantic possibilities between the Archer and the Goat, let's think for a moment about the influence of the ruling planet on an individual's sun sign.

Sagittarius is ruled by Jupiter, the planet of expansion, optimism, good fortune, and abundance. This affects the Sagittarian personality. It gives the Archer her footloose freedom and allows her to trust in luck. After all, she has more than her fair share of it, and gambling frequently pays off handsomely.

But Capricorn is ruled by Saturn, the planet of obstacles, limitation, restriction, and discipline. This can seem dreary to the Archer, but there are great benefits to Saturn's stern influence. For one thing, Saturn-ruled people usually finish what they start. (Do Sagittarians?) Their determination and patience are legendary, and they typically stick it out, no matter what, while typical Sagittarius women have a short fuse and tend to lack staying power. The Goat seeks social approval and prestige; the Archer-woman laughs at such things.

This is a couple that can truly learn from each other. They are at opposite ends of a continuum … and perhaps both would be better off if they moved a bit toward the center. If the Archer can lighten up the Goat, both would probably be happier. And if the Capricorn man could convince the Sagittarius woman of the pleasure of producing long-term results, she might feel more attached to Earth and all it offers.

The Sagittarius woman is thrilled by the possibility of adventure. A love affair with a Capricorn man could be viewed as a quest for insight into other ways of life. If the Archer believes this, she may find a world of unforeseen opportunities with a Capricorn man.

Sagittarius Woman/
Aquarius Man

The Archer has a wide reputation as a freedom lover, right? Well, it's no secret that her status as the most footloose member of the zodiac is met (and often exceeded) by the typical Aquarius man.

Of course, their reasons for a shared obsession with the cosmic route to total freedom are different. His is altruistic, and hers is more (dare we say it?) selfish. The Water Bearer wants to save the world;

the Archer-woman is primarily interested in securing herself enough wide-open space to operate. But this independent approach puts them both on the same romantic wavelength—so the fun begins. And for this couple, it never has to end.

Since they are restless, social spirits, the Archer and the Water Bearer can typically hold their own in any crowd, at any hour, and in any place, no matter how offbeat. The Aquarius man loves eccentricity and the Sagittarius woman was born to explore, so they come alive when they're in unusual environments and there's plenty of mischief to get into. Both tend to be idealists, which applies to romance too. They want their love affair to be a shining example of openheartedness and communication.

To be verbally and intellectually entwined is often more important to these two than physical passion—although they will usually share plenty of both. With the Aquarius man's emotional detachment and the Sagittarius woman's no-strings attitude, true intimacy may be slow to develop. And the Water Bearer's stubborn streak will clash with the female Archer's bossiness from time to time. When it does, she's more likely to budge than he is—and quicker to forget the bumps too.

But this is a match with the potential for romantic greatness, and both have the drive and the zeal to make it real.

Sagittarius Woman/ Pisces Man

The female Archer is on a quest for wisdom and spiritual fulfillment; the Fish seems to have all the answers. She tends to be intrigued by his mystery; he is often inspired by her high energy and directness. She responds to his sensuality; he is charmed by her jovial nature and her optimism.

These may be pieces of the cosmic puzzle that draw the Sagittarius woman and the Pisces man together. Their attraction is logical and sensual, and there's a powerful sexual magnetism that simply cannot be ignored. So nobody's asking what compels these two to get together. But farther down the road of romance, more than one Sagittarius/Pisces couple has asked themselves why they should stay together!

The primary challenge of the love match between the Archer-woman and the Fish is this: He tends to be dependent, emotionally needy, and somewhat introverted. If his romantic dreams are not fulfilled (and truthfully, that doesn't easily happen), he may lapse into a depression or some dramatic display of self-pity.

The female Archer tends to feel trapped by the emotional demands of her partner. When the Fish starts whining about commitment (particularly if he does it too soon, and he probably will), the Sagittarius woman may suddenly notice that his emotional waters are not only dark but murky. Her fiery spirit may feel extinguished. And she often loses patience with the Pisces man because of his basic shyness. She blazes in, and she often feels she needs a partner who eggs her on rather than holds her back.

The philosopher in her loves the poet in him, and her fiery passion nicely complements his watery sensuality, but the qualities that stabilize a love relationship over the long term are weak in this Sagittarius/Pisces match. Proceed with romantic caution!

Fiery Sagittarius Woman

BETTE MIDLER
b. December 1, 1945

The typical Sagittarius woman is born with energy and ambition. She's on a quest for experience and wisdom, and she's ready, willing, and able to blaze her own unique trail.

Enter Sagittarian Bette Midler. Born in Hawaii, an earthly paradise (as Jupiterian luck would have it), she was named for the actress Bette Davis. She landed her first movie role—as an extra in the film *Hawaii*—while still a drama student at the University of Hawaii.

This taste of the entertainment business drew her to New York, where she made her Broadway debut as Tzeitel in *Fiddler on the Roof.* But unconventional Bette's next career move was to a men's bathhouse! There, she assumed her new stage identity—the Divine Miss M—and captivated her audience, even if they were dressed in towels!

From this offbeat launching pad to stardom, Bette landed a contract in 1972 with Atlantic records, and she won a Grammy Award for Best New Artist. Next, she collected a Tony Award for her appearance at the Palace Theater. Her musical revues and television specials (such as *Clams on the Half Shell* and *Ol' Red Hair Is Back*) won her worldwide fame (and an Emmy), and her record and album releases shot off the charts.

But like the typical Archer, she was poised for even greater honors. In 1979, she won an Academy Award nomination for her film debut in *The Rose*. She found a cinematic home in comedy, starring in such classics as *Down and Out in Beverly Hills*, *Ruthless People*, and *The First Wives Club*.

Hit records, movies, her own production company, musical awards, cross-country tours, sold-out engagements at Radio City Music Hall—Bette Midler has had them all! And she manages a marriage (to Martin von Haselberg) and motherhood too. Each of her Sagittarian arrows flies ever higher: The sky is the limit for the Divine Miss M.